all
color
book
of
Birds

Octopus

Octopus Books

First published in 1972 by
Octopus Books Limited
59 Grosvenor Street, London W 1

ISBN 7064 0124 7
Distributed in the USA by Crescent Books,
a Division of Crown Publishers, Inc.

©Octopus Books Limited
Filmset by Yendall and Company Ltd., London
Produced by Mandarin Publishers
Printed in Hong Kong

Contents

Well-known and Rare Birds

There are certain birds in every continent which are known to practically everyone whether they are interested in birds or not and these are also high among those species which are the most numerous in the world. In Europe the Starlings, Sparrows, closely followed by the Tits, Thrushes and Blackbirds are probably the best known; while the Americans would probably pick out the Chickadees and some of the Grosbeaks which are frequent visitors to bird tables, and the Turkey Vultures are familiar to travellers on the American continent. South Americans would instantly recognize some of the Tanagers, and in Australia birds like the Roseate Cockatoo, popularly known as the Galah, and the ubiquitous Willie Wagtail have invaded the towns in much the same way as the Pigeons have in Europe. The Little Blue Penguin is also well-known in Southern Australia, since it is a major tourist attraction there when it leaves its burrow to go to the sea to fish. Finally in Africa, there are various Ibises whose voices are very well-known, and some of the Weavers are familiar, particularly the Quelea, which destroys so many of the crops and is such a nuisance that its nests are systematically blown up by the authorities.

There are, however, plenty of species that are extremely numerous but which are not particularly well-known. This is often because of their chosen habitat; for instance Wilson's Petrel, which breeds in vast colonies in the Antarctic and is extremely widespread in the off season, has been considered as being one of the most numerous species. On the other hand, it is extremely difficult to assess with any great accuracy the numbers of such birds, since they spend most of their time out at sea.

Other birds are very familiar to a great many people because of their appearance in zoos all over the world. Penguins are much loved, probably because of their amusing ability to caricature human mannerisms, and as their natural habitat is in the cold southern seas and the Antarctica, few people would know of them if they had not been successfully kept and bred in the northern hemisphere. Peacocks, parrots and the more colourful tropical birds are also a familiar sight in zoos, as are Pelicans and Ostriches.

There are unfortunately too many birds whose numbers are decreasing steadily and which are consequently termed as rare, and in spite of an increasing awareness in the world today of the danger of extinction of many species and the need for protection, the list of rare birds grows daily. The reason for this is largely because of the destruction of particular kinds of habitat which are the homes of species that cannot adapt to any other way of life. Marshes, swamps and wetlands used to abound in Europe and Asia and housed vast flocks of many different kinds of birds; such areas are now few and far between as they have been reclaimed for either agricultural or building purposes. A few birds have managed to adapt to living in the changed world of the twentieth century, for example, the Black Redstart is now to be found in most large cities in western Europe, although it was previously one of the rarer birds of the cliffs and rocky countryside. Fortunately it does not seem to see any difference between a cliff and the side of an ancient building or factory. And very occasionally a species thought to be extinct is rediscovered —the Cahow, or Bermuda Petrel is one example and the noisy Scrub Bird of Australia is another more recently discovered near Perth. But on the whole the story is one of the failure of birds whose particular habitats or food is being destroyed, to adapt to other conditions.

The birds of prey are a group which are suffering in this way, largely because they are regularly shot and their eggs taken by gamekeepers in the mistaken belief that they all kill game birds. The European Short-toed Eagle for instance, lives solely on snakes and lizards but is now disappearing as a result of persistent shooting. The Monkey-eating Eagle of the Philippines is one of the largest and most powerful of the birds of prey and as its name suggests, catches monkeys; unfortunately it is fast disappearing due to the destruction of much of the forest in which it lives and also due to the great demand for the birds in foreign zoos. In America the national emblem, the Bald Eagle, the Californian Condor and the Everglade Kite of Florida are all in danger of disappearing and in Britain the Peregrine and the Kestrel are declining in numbers. Many of the chemicals used on the land are thought to be responsible for infertile eggs and for poisoning the birds.

Other birds suffer from man's demands; thousands of small song-birds are killed every year as delicacies for gourmets, while others are trapped for the cage-bird trade. Many of the seabirds and the water-fowl die in their hundreds on the beaches of America and Britain because their wings are covered with the oil discharged into the sea by tankers. Bird Protection Societies do their best to rescue the birds and clean their wings, but inevitably the majority of them die. Yet more birds are the victims of animals that have been introduced to new places by man like cats, rats and pigs, and which subsequently run wild and kill off vast numbers of nesting seabirds— this has happened on Ascension Island and on the Pacific and Caribbean islands, and the birds consequently do not return and are increasingly limited in their breeding grounds and habitats.

In most parts of the world reserves and sanctuaries have been set aside for the protection of rare birds and and although these do a very good job they are hampered by lack of funds and lack of co-operation from those who are busy destroying habitats and the birds themselves. Some birds have captured the popular imagination, such as the Whooping Crane in North America, and its protection has resulted from public concern about its fate; but the Siberian White Crane and Japanese Crested Ibis have not been so lucky in attracting sympathy in their parts of the world. On the whole nearly all the rare birds have declined so drastically in numbers because of man's encroachment, and all of them could be saved if those who could provide the funds were interested. However, the World Wildlife Fund has been very successful in its appeals and is bringing to the notice of an increasing number of people all over the world the importance of conserving vanishing wildlife in every country.

Previous page: left Two fat little Blue Tits busily searching for insects and grubs . . . these friendly and acrobatic birds belong to a family of sixty five odd species including the North American Chickadees, and they are among the most popular of all well-known birds. They are always curious and pert and relatively unafraid of humans—in fact they are easy to tame and teach simple tricks. Many species nest in nest boxes, and Blue Tits are notoriously unfussy about where they build; old cans, boots, letterboxes, pipes and car radiators have all been used.

Right One of the best known birds throughout the world is probably the Budgerigar. They are found in the wild in arid scrubland areas of the interior of Australia, and have been bred in captivity in a vast range of colours and colour combinations—though the colour of these two is their natural colour in the wild. They are easy to keep and will live in captivity for many years.

Left Just as the Kiwi is associated with New Zealand, so the Kookaburra is with Australia, where it is very well-known. One of the largest of the Kingfisher family, the Kookaburra has a number of weird, human-sounding cries which has earned it the name of the Laughing Jackass. The birds give a loud, raucous chorus as they go to roost in the tree tops at dusk and then again at dawn, so that they are also known as the 'Bushman's Clock'.

Bottom left The Blue Jay is found in most of eastern North America and is a common bird which often visits bird tables. Their harsh calls are a well-known sound as they argue with each other over food, and they are also able to mimic the calls of a number of other birds. A characteristic of the family is a crest which the bird raises when angry or excited, and this bird has raised his crest at the approach of the photographer.

Right Of all British birds the Robin is the one instantly recognized by everybody. They have great character and although they are curious and friendly towards humans they can be extremely aggressive towards other Robins or red-breasted birds that come anywhere near their own particular territories in the breeding season. The American Robin is also very well-known, but is not the same species, being more like a Blackbird in appearance.

Above One of the most picturesque and delicately coloured of the world's birds, Flamingoes never fail to fascinate those who see them. These Lesser Flamingoes are some of almost countless thousands that nest by the East African lakes where they are joined in winter by large flocks of migrating Greater Flamingoes.

Left The common Pigeons which are almost taken for granted in all large cities in Europe are descended from the Rock Dove, and are nearly always domestic pigeons gone wild. As this pigeon shows, their plumage when seen close to is very beautiful, but the overall effect is not particularly striking.

Right 'Black-headed' is really a misnomer for this pretty gull, as the attractive hood that is part of the breeding plumage is chocolate brown in colour. They are extremely abundant throughout Europe and can be seen in huge flocks on the coast, along rivers and far inland following the plough. Although perhaps the most numerous of any species of gull, they are not necessarily better known than the Herring Gull, which is always to be seen by the sea and is very conspicuous as it scavenges noisily for food.

Top left The smallest of the Penguins is the Fairy, Little or Little Blue Penguin of Australia, New Zealand and the nearby Chatham Islands. They nest in burrows and crevices, and frequently choose sites under coastal bungalows. They feed at night and go off to the sea from their burrows in large groups to fish; the sight is a major tourist attraction and in some places special floodlights have been set up to show the little birds struggling back up the beach after their expedition.

Centre left A very fluffy Hedge Sparrow sitting in a Spindle bush on a cold winter's day. It is a typical garden bird in Britain though not so common or well-known as the House Sparrow, being less numerous, much shyer and also rather more attractive.

Below After the Ostrich the Emu is the largest bird in the world, standing about six feet high. They are widespread in Australia and are considered a pest because they graze the grass wanted for sheep and also eat and break down the crops. Large numbers are still reported in parts of Australia in spite of the fact that they have been hunted and shot ever since the days of the early settlers.

Right The colourful Gang-gang Cockatoo is found in the Australian Alps, and although it is not uncommon in some parts it is steadily decreasing over most of its range. It lives in heavily wooded areas and is quite tame, therefore being easy prey for hunters.

Above The noisy gatherings of Starlings in the centres of large cities in Europe and in most parts of the world where they have been introduced, are a familiar sight though few people know that only 150 years ago they were rare birds in Britain and Europe. There are various species of Starlings, and these two are in fact Superb Starlings photographed in Africa where they live.

Left The Toucans' amazing beaks, sometimes almost as big as their bodies, make them one of the most unmistakable of all bird families. They are found in the wild only in tropical forests in the Americas and are particularly numerous in the Amazon region. The reason for the size and startling colour of their beaks is not known, but the birds' comical appearance is enhanced by their playful habits. They are very noisy, and chatter to one another with harsh chuckles interspersed with the hollow clacking of their beaks. They often fence together with their beaks and toss berries into the air or to each other, seemingly from general *joie de vivre*.

Right More gorgeous birds from the tropical rainforests of Central and South America . . . the Macaws are the kings of the Parrot family and are frequently seen in zoos. This is a pair of Scarlet Macaws, not quite as magnificent as the Red and Green Macaws perhaps, but still very striking.

Above The Siberian White Crane breeds in three widely separated regions in northern Asia and migrates to winter in particular spots in China, India and the region of the southern Caspian Sea. Although it is now an extremely rare species, it is protected over most of its range and can be bred successfully in zoos so that it should be safe from extinction.

Left Two Rothschild's Mynas which come from the Indonesian island of Bali. In one way these birds are well-known because they have been in great demand as captive birds but this demand has depleted the number of wild birds so much that they are now rare in their wild state. They are very handsome birds, pure white except for black tips to the wings and tail and a patch of bare, blue skin around the eye.

Right is another bird which is now a little less rare than it was due to protection. The Japanese or Manchurian Crane breeds in Japan and eastern Siberia, though it used to range over a much wider area. In Japan it is fully protected as it is considered a sign of good luck and long life whenever it visits someone's land, and it appears frequently in Japanese legends and history.

Left This magnificent looking bird uses its strong, curved beak to catch and eat monkeys, and it is called after this rather unusual taste in food . . . the Monkey-eating Eagle lives in the deep forests of the Philippines and is becoming alarmingly rare due to the steady destruction of its habitat.

Below A family of beautiful Trumpeter Swans at their nest in western North America. These large birds are a splendid example of the 'rescue' of a vanishing species. They were at one time in danger of dying out because of the destruction of their breeding grounds, and because of persistent shooting. However, strict federal protection, helpful public co-operation and the establishment of a number of sanctuaries have brought the numbers up beyond the danger point and breeding Trumpeters are now quite a common sight in several National Parks.

Right The Black Swan of Australia and Tasmania is a particularly handsome bird with its black, curly feathers, bright red bill and attractive white tips to its wings (the latter only show when the bird is flying). It was discovered by the Dutch in 1697 and was subsequently made the emblem of the armorial standard of Western Australia. The Dutch took it to Europe where a black swan was regarded with amazement, and it has been a popular bird ever since.

Seabirds

Seabirds form one of the most interesting groups of birds, and one that is also not very well-known since many people do not have the chance to observe birds which spend most of their time out at sea. There is some controversy over just what species of birds may be classed as seabirds, as some families can be treated as either landbirds or seabirds, but on the whole it is agreed that there are four main families and about 285 species. This is a small proportion of the total number of species known at the present time (about 8,600), but many of the seabirds have enormous populations, and their colonies can consist of millions of birds, while some of them are among the commonest birds in the world.

Obviously the birds come ashore to breed, but for the rest of the year they prefer to wander the world's oceans, or remain over the sea even if near the shore. This is because they all feed from the surface of the sea, either on seaplankton or on fish and other sea animals which only exist where there is plankton, and plankton itself only forms as a result of the presence of certain salts and minerals. There are some areas where there is virtually no movement at all in the water and they do not produce sufficient plankton to support sea life and consequently the

birds. Seabirds are, however, to be found on most seas and the Pacific Ocean is the home of the majority of the birds usually classed as seabirds, followed by the Atlantic and then the smaller oceans.

One of the commonest birds is Wilson's Petrel, a small bird of the tube nosed variety about the size of the British Blackbird. It breeds in the Antarctic and on the small islands to the north in huge colonies totalling many millions of birds. During the Antarctic winter it moves further north and wanders over the oceans as far up as the North Atlantic and is very common on the eastern coasts of America. The Short-tailed Shearwater, which breeds off southern Australia and then migrates in a great figure of eight route across the Pacific, also occurs in large numbers. On the other hand some seabirds are very rare. The Cahow or Bermuda Petrel breeds only on an island off Bermuda where there are no more than about a score of pairs. This is partly because it suffers from the effects of DDT, which has contaminated the seas and is passed on to the birds through the zooplankton on which they feed.

Penguins must be one of the best known birds of all, as their amusing and very human characteristics make them among the most popular creatures at zoos. In fact they are being

seen there at a disadvantage, since they are supremely suited to life in the water and can propel themselves along at speeds of up to twenty five miles per hour: it is their ungainly waddling and hopping on land that often makes them so entertaining. All species of Penguins live in the Southern Hemisphere and the largest is the Emperor Penguin, some four feet in length, while the smallest, the Fairy Penguin (which is found along the coast of southern Australia) is only a foot high. They are highly gregarious and nest in huge colonies, the Emperor Penguins sometimes huddling together in great packs to conserve warmth as they incubate their single eggs on top of their feet.

The Albatrosses are also familiar to many, at least by name. The Wandering Albatross has the largest wingspan of any bird alive today. From wingtip to wingtip it measures up to twelve feet—a really majestic bird as it glides for hours on the air currents created over the oceans by the troughs in the waves. They are seabirds in the true sense of the word, spending months on end wandering over the southern oceans, thousands of miles from land. No wonder that sailors regarded them as omens of storms and gales, for they are almost helpless without the wind and are complete masters of it. On land they are extremely awkward, and seemingly quite fearless of men; clumsily landing on the decks of ships, they are unable to rise up again and earned their names of 'Gooneys' and 'Mollymawks', meaning foolish gulls.

Many different species, including the Skuas (with the exception of the Great Skua), Gulls, Terns, and Auks are only found in the Northern Hemisphere. Auks are interesting and comical birds and mostly live in the Pacific where they breed on the rocky coasts and islands, spending the winter further out at sea. Like Penguins they are plump, mainly black and white in colour with bright red, blue and yellow 'extras' in some species. The Atlantic Puffin is the real clown of the family; always inquisitive and poking its nose into its neighbours' business, it stands at the entrance to its nest burrow and watches the goings-on around it with an eye of apparent disdain. They are also quarrelsome and use their large bills to grab an opponent's leg, the two birds fighting so hard that they sometimes fall over the cliff-edge before letting go of each other.

Gulls are for the most part hardly seabirds at all. The Kittiwake is probably the one most entitled to be called a seabird, while most of the others are frequently seen inland and some nest hundreds of miles from the coast. The Terns often nest in similar sites to the Gulls but then move further out to sea after the breeding season. The related Skuas or Jaegers are all piratical in their habits. The Great Skua is perhaps the worst scavenger as it frequently follows ships and fishing fleets and chases Gulls and Terns until they drop the food they are carrying. It also tends to nest close to Penguin colonies so as to be ready to pounce on any unguarded eggs or chicks.

The nesting colonies of some of the seabirds can be a startling and impressive sight, and watching thousands of birds gathered together on a sea cliff or on the shore, all nesting within a few inches of each other and chattering and quarrelling, is an unforgettable experience. Some of the smallest seabirds such as Shearwaters and Petrels nest in burrows in the peaty soil often found near the sea, and again hundreds of burrows can be found close together to which the birds return after spending the day searching for food far out to sea.

Although many of these magnificent seabirds will never be seen by most people there are occasions when individuals are blown inshore by gales and can be seen outside their usual range, and sometimes large flocks of birds are driven eastwards when migrating south and are 'wrecked' along the western shores of Europe.

Previous page: left Tropicbirds are particularly graceful birds and this Red-billed Tropicbird is found in the New World around the tropical coasts of the Caribbean, Central America and the Galapagos Islands. They are very aggressive and have fierce battles between themselves, when eggs and young often get destroyed or lost in the fighting. They are also called 'Bo's'n-birds' because of their high call notes, which resemble the sound made by a boatswain's pipe.

Right The largest member of the Shearwater family is the Giant Petrel, known to the southern sailors and fishermen as the 'Nelly' or 'Stinker'. These birds are strong and graceful flyers and skim effortlessly over the sea as their name suggests, but they are unattractive in their appearance and their habits.

Right American White Pelicans nest along the lakes from British Columbia and Ontario south to Texas. The birds are famous for the remarkable pouches underneath their beaks which can hold up to three gallons, and act as a temporary 'larder' which the birds fill when out fishing.

Top left A Cormorant beats its wings on the surface of the water in order to clean them. Although they are classed as seabirds many species live inland on rivers and lakes and they are never far from land even when living on the coast. They catch fish by diving from the surface of the water, and they are credited with being able to dive to great depths, though on the whole they prefer to fish in shallow water. An amusing characteristic of theirs is sitting on a rock with their wings held out to dry in a heraldic position.

Bottom left A Black-browed Albatross commenting on the world as it sits on its nest. . . . These birds have been nick-named 'Gooneys' or 'Mollymawks' because of their stupidity and comic ways. No amount of contact seems to teach them to fear man and their eggs can easily be stolen. Their courtship displays are famous and involve grotesque dances accompanied by much bowing and scraping, snapping of bills and groaning noises.

Right Of all seabirds Emperor Penguins must be the only ones which never set foot on land. Largest of all the Penguins, they breed only on the coasts of the Antarctic continent and gather in large assemblies called 'rookeries' on the sea ice.

Below Two Rockhopper Penguins argue over territories in a colony on the Falkland Islands. These Penguins breed on the Antarctic continent and many islands as far north as Tristan da Cunha. They are so named because of the way in which they leap about on land, and in many ways they are the most comical of the Penguin family.

Top left A Manx Shearwater outside its burrow. These attractive birds are found throughout the European North Atlantic waters and are very accurate long distance flyers (see the chapter on Migration). They are close relatives of the Short-tailed Shearwater, or Mutton-bird, who is also a great traveller and provides the islands off Australia with a considerable source of income, as they are caught in large numbers and canned as 'Tasmanian Squab'. The down is used in sleeping bags and their stomach oil in cosmetics and drugs.

Centre left A Northern Gannet and its chick showing the strong, streamlined beak which is typical of the Gannet family. A particularly dramatic sight is a group of Gannets feeding. Wheeling above shoals of fish, these beautiful 'modern-looking' birds dive for their food from a height of fifty to a hundred feet and hit the water with a resounding splash, throwing spray anything up to ten feet into the air. They emerge a moment later, having caught and swallowed the fish under water, and take off ready for the next dive.

Bottom left A delightful group of Caspian Terns at their nest. There are some thirty nine species of Terns which are found all over the world, and the Caspian Tern is one of the largest and has a particularly wide range, being only absent as a breeding species from South America. They are easily distinguishable from gulls by their slender build, long wings, forked tails and manner of flight.

Right Hundreds of Common Guillemot huddle together on narrow ledges in a precipice facing the sea. They are incubating their eggs, which are laid on the bare rock and are pear-shaped in order to stop them rolling off the edge if they are dislodged.

Display

Most people have seen a male Peacock raising his beautiful, long feathers off the ground into an enormous fan, but they do not always realize that he is displaying his special ornamental feathers on purpose to attract a mate. Many other birds besides Peacocks perform intricate and beautiful displays and have wonderfully coloured extra feathers specially for their dances. These feathers are often part of the tail or wings, and are usually brightly coloured, or strangely shaped, or even take the form of plumes and ruffs coming from odd parts of the body. Some like the Frigate-bird, or the Sage Grouse, have air sacks which they inflate; others repeat extraordinary noises and song sequences when displaying and a few construct special places, like the Bowerbirds, or clear particular patches of ground completely bare for their dances. Many birds display in flight and give wonderful performances of diving, wheeling and aerial gymnastics often accompanied by special mating cries or 'sound effects'. Snipe, for example, spread out their tails in a fan as they dive towards the ground and the air going through their feathers makes a loud drumming noise. The lucky females for whose benefit all this is done are often themselves very dully plumaged and in general take little interest in the various performances of their prospective mates.

It is the many species of male Birds of Paradise which have the most remarkable special feathers of all as they cover the most astonishing range of colours and shapes. The birds usually display by dancing on a branch and then flinging their plumes over their heads. The plumes sometimes take the form of long tail wires, or head plumes which may be twice as long as the bird, or thick fan-like plumes normally hidden under the wings which are puffed out and spread round the bird like a cloak.

The Lyrebirds that live in the forest and scrub of eastern Australia also have beautiful display feathers and create suitable surroundings to show them off. The male establishes a large territory for himself where he has a series of display grounds. He visits each special area in turn throughout the day and builds large mounds of damp earth on which he performs his magnificent antics. Starting with a selection from his wonderful repertoire of songs and noises (Lyrebirds are also famous for their powers of mimicry) he then slowly unfolds his tail, raising it up over his back and head until it covers him completely and the tips of the lacy feathers are touching the ground. This is the climax of his performance, and after a few moments he stalks off into the bush. He takes no part in the nest building and bringing up of the young, like most of the elaborate displayers.

Some species gather together in large numbers to display and attract females, and their display sites are called leks. Male Black Grouse, known as Blackcocks, meet at their traditional leks in a meadow or on open moorland usually at dawn in spring and early summer, and then display in their own individual territories called 'courts'. Much fighting goes on at the boundaries, and the birds strut about with wings drooped and tails raised into spikey fans to show the white under-tail feathers. The throat and chest are puffed out and the air sacks inflated, and they sometimes make short flights into the air accompanied by hissing and crowing noises. The females do not take much notice at first, and join the males after a few weeks. Their arrival is greeted with much excitement by the males, but it is only after half a dozen visits that the females are ready to mate. The Blackcocks continue to display to each other while the female goes off to build a nest and lay her eggs without the help of a mate—males of many species which are gorgeously coloured or have splendid display feathers with which to perform usually make very bad husbands, and in fact pairs are rarely formed.

The Bowerbirds of Australia have remarkable display habits since the males build bowers, or avenues of twigs as part of their courtship. The Gardener Bowerbird constructs a bower rather like a small native hut out of thousands of twigs stuck into the ground, and then, not content with that, he lays out a garden all round it of shells and flower petals, tending it almost daily. The Satin Bowerbird of eastern Australia, although not much bigger than a Jackdaw, may pile his twigs and sticks anything up to nine feet high, and then paint them with masticated fruit pulp and anything else colourful that he can find. All the males are

dully plumaged birds, which is perhaps why they work so extraordinarily hard to attract a mate. They are undoubtedly the most advanced technicians below man in the animal kingdom, and it is curious that the male birds' remarkable skill is not used to build the nest—the female does this and rears the young alone.

Most birds that form pairs continue to display to each other for a long time and strengthen the pair bond by mutual preening and feeding on the nest. This is particularly conspicuous among birds that nest in large colonies—obviously the temptation to run off with other mates is much greater when there are hundreds of nests next door to each other!

Birds also give very impressive displays of anger and aggression, as those which have territories or which form pairs will fiercely protect their property and challenge any rivals who come near their chosen mates. Females will defend the nest and young against other birds and predators, and often hiss, grunt or make unusual cries and shrieks to intimidate the enemy. They will even go to considerable lengths to distract enemies by fluttering and hobbling about as if injured, sometimes dragging a wing pretending that it is broken until they have led the enemy well away from the nest or young. Both male and female Plovers are adept at feigning injury and causing a distraction if danger threatens, and a female Mallard will splash across a pool to draw a predator after herself and away from her brood.

Song plays an important part in all these displays, and courtship songs serve the double purpose of attracting a mate and announcing the ownership of a territory. The Robin, which is seen in most English gardens and which is often very tame, can be extremely fierce since it is a very territorially minded bird, and will attack any intruders long and furiously—even stuffed Robins put there on purpose. Although birds usually only attack other members of their own species which come into their territories, it is interesting that Nightingales will attack a Cuckoo if given the chance—they must know it is the idle parasite that lays its eggs in the nests of other birds.

Previous page: left The Sage Grouse is a native of North America and its display habits are similar to those of the Black Grouse. The males appearance is more dramatic than that of the Black-cocks since their tails are larger and darker in colour and form a magnificent spikey fan, while their air sacks in the side of the neck are covered with a thick ruff of white, ornamental feathers which looks like a long feather boa.

Right A Dotterel photographed while trying to distract the intruder away from its family. It is pretending to be ill and unable to walk, and may even continue the performance until the intruder is so close that it can attack with its beak. The display is typical of the Plover family, though more often the birds pretend to have a broken wing.

Top left Owls are some of the most aggressive of all birds and this young Long-eared Owl has already learned all the tricks of intimidation—puffing out the feathers makes him seem twice the size, glaring eyes with the pupils dilated, arched wings and much hissing and snapping of his bill make him a formidable opponent, even though the effect is slightly marred by all his baby fluff.

Bottom left A Great Crested Grebe on its nest raises its crest and stands up to attack a rival which has invaded its territory and come too close. This is really an extension of its courtship display, as they are not at all aggressive in the face of danger. They hide instead, and sink slowly beneath the surface until only their heads can be seen, and they often swim about for some time like submarines.

Right One of the most beautiful sights in the world of birds is that of a Peacock displaying. . . . The ornamental feathers are not, as is often thought, part of the tail, but come from its base, and each one has the silky branches, the black tips and the glorious 'eyes' that make them individually quite outstanding.

Above Vociferous greetings between two Fulmars. . . . This ceremony is performed all through the breeding season and it is common among seabirds which nest in colonies on the cliffs around the coast. These are two Northern Fulmars, a species that has undergone an intriguing increase in European waters over the last hundred years, so that during this time the birds have occupied virtually every sea cliff in Great Britain.

Left The owner of this incredible structure has departed in search of more decoration—and collecting together so many twigs and shells is a full time occupation for the male Bowerbird and takes him several weeks. This is the partly finished bower of one of the nine species of avenue builders which are considered to be the most specialized architects of the entire family.

Right A male Superb Lyrebird displaying. This posture is in fact much more typical than the one familiar from Australian postage stamps which shows the tail erect and spread into a perfect lyre—the tail is like this only for a few moments during the courtship display. The frame of the 'lyre' is formed by the outer pair of tail feathers, beautifully banded and curved with distinctive round black tips, while the 'strings' are the inner quills, which are brown above and white below and have a delicate, lacy texture.

Left Ruffs are waders which are directly named after their extraordinary display plumage. In springtime the males develop pointed ear tufts and a large collar, or ruff, round their necks which they expand when displaying to the females, and which can be virtually any colour from black to white. When courting the birds perform a weird little dance and point their beaks to the ground while blowing up their ruffs and quivering all over.

Below An air sack to beat all air sacks in both size and colour . . . the male Frigate-bird sits by the nest site he has chosen and inflates his pouch for hours on end in order to attract a mate. Normally the pouch is a dull orange colour but during the mating season it turns bright red. 'Man-'o-war' birds, as sailors call them, spend their lives on the wing, soaring and wheeling over the tropical seas.

Right This spectacular Crowned Crane lives in Africa and, like all Cranes, has a wonderful dancing ceremony. Both sexes partake in the displays which continue all the year round. The birds walk stiffly round each other with wings half spread, or leap in the air; this is interspersed with deep bowings and stretchings and playful games with pieces of grass and twigs.

Nests

Birds' nests are perhaps one of the most remarkable things in the world of living creatures—and although some birds hardly bother to prepare at all for their young, others build nests of almost unbelievable intricacy involving days of work and demanding great skill. One of these birds is the small Sociable Weaver which builds a vast complex in company with hundreds of other weavers. Another is the Tailorbird, one of the Warbler family which is very appropriately named. It selects two large leaves, punctures holes down the edges, and then stuffs hairs and fluff through them so that they are sewn together to form a pocket which will then hold the nest proper.

At the other extreme, the King Penguin makes no nest at all. It simply lays an egg and sits on it. Practically every species that builds a nest constructs something different, so there are innumerable types of nests of all shapes, sizes and structures. However, the 'basic' pattern, of which there are infinite varieties, is the cup shaped nest made of twigs and grasses, with additional materials like moss, leaves, spiders' webs and mud to strengthen it, and then feathers and down to make a soft, warm lining which will exactly fit the shape of the bird. These are the nests built by the well-known Thrushes, Blackbirds, Robins and

many of the songbirds, and can be found in trees, hedges, on the ground and sometimes woven into branches and twigs with plant stalks to prevent them falling to the ground.

The Social Weaver of South Africa is one of the species that has brought social development to its highest point in the bird kingdom—their communal nests are sometimes ten feet high and fifteen feet wide and often mistaken for a native hut. The roof is a waterproof straw thatch, under which each pair of birds build their own nest with its long entrance tube and soft lining. Other species weave separate nests, and the Village Weaver builds a framework of palm leaves before weaving the flask-shaped nest.

Some nests are made entirely of mud. Those of Swallows and House Martins are probably familiar to most people, although not everybody is lucky enough to see the birds working away sticking each beakful of mud on to the last until the nest is complete. Australian Mudlarks are particularly skilled and build a perfectly shaped bowl of mud mixed with bits of plants which is balanced on a horizontal branch, while the Ovenbird of South America constructs a spherical home with an entrance at the side. The Swift family all have a special type of saliva with which they stick the mud together,

and it is often mixed with bits of plant and vegetable matter. Bird's nest soup is made from the nests of certain Asian Swiflets. These nests are entirely made of the birds' own salivary secretion, unmixed with feathers or leaves, and are very highly prized. Palm Swifts are perhaps the most remarkable since they merely glue a very small pad of feathers to the underside of a palm leaf and then glue on their eggs as well and incubate them clinging upright to the leaf with their claws.

Camouflage is an important element in nest building, and many of the water birds' nests look just like a heap of floating twigs and rubbish. The parents take great care to cover the eggs with leaves and reeds when they leave the nest to hide them from enemies. Some of these nests are actually floating, others are more carefully built and are anchored to water plants and the Grebe's nest has in addition a small cup on the top of the mound.

Many birds are not as industrious as all the songbirds and waterfowl, and simply bore a hole in a tree or into the earth, or just use a natural hole as a nest. Tits, Kingfishers, Bee-eaters, Woodpeckers and Barbets, Hornbills, Shearwaters and a host of others do this, and some of them line the hole with feathers and dried grass, others just lay their eggs on the floor of a chamber at the end of the tunnel. Hornbills—birds from Africa, Asia and India, which all have enormous down-curved bills and large eyelashes—have unusual nesting habits in that the female is sealed up inside the hole while sitting on the eggs, and is fed by the male through the tiny slit that is left. Presumably this voluntary incarceration is to ensure maximum protection against snakes and monkeys.

Game birds and many waders nest in shallow scrapes in the ground, which they either find or make by shuffling about until they have created a hollow. Terns do this, usually in colonies, and eventually build up a kind of nest by throwing

back onto the eggs when they leave anything that they have managed to reach while sitting. Fairy Terns however, build no nest at all and just lay one egg on a branch of a tree—nor do they care when the eggs and young fall off, which they frequently do!

There is a unique group of birds called Megapodes which live in Australia and Malaya and which do not incubate their eggs themselves. One of these, the Mallee Fowl of the Australian bush, builds a huge mound of sand and rotting vegetation, lays a large number of eggs in a hole dug in the middle, and then leaves the mound to generate enough heat to incubate the eggs. The male attends to it regularly and has a heat-sensitive lining to his beak which enables him to test the temperature of the mound by tasting the soil—experiments have shown that he keeps the temperature at a constant heat of about 92°F while the eggs are incubating. This method of incubation is really remarkable and unique in the bird world—nor is there any apparent reason why the Mallee Fowl cannot sit on a nest like any other bird. The chicks on hatching have to fight their way to the surface of the mound, and their parents take no notice of them thereafter—obviously all their energy is exhausted incubating the eggs.

Nests are sometimes used for years in succession, being repaired each spring—Golden Eagles and some Vultures often have huge nests of sticks piled up over the years. The colourful Love Birds and Waxbills which range from Africa to Australia don't bother to build their own nests and use old ones of the Weaverbirds, and of course, the last word in idleness is the well-known Cuckoo which is notorious for dropping its eggs in other nests and leaving an already over worked and usually smaller bird, like a Robin, to bring up the young—newly hatched Cuckoos have even been known to roll out the eggs and chicks of their host as soon as they are born!

Previous page: left It is possibly the large family of Wood Warblers that give American bird watchers more pleasure than any other, particularly in spring when the woods are alive with flocks of these little bright coloured birds. Nest building is done almost entirely by the female and it is a very well-made and solid structure.

Right A Great Reed Warbler clings to one of the reeds which supports the nest before feeding its young. The nest is made of sedges, reeds and small roots and lined with soft down from water plants. The photograph shows how it is woven round several strong standing reeds and is thus suspended above the water.

Top left A Kingfisher returns to its nest in the river bank with a fish half as long as itself. These jewel-like birds burrow long tunnels, sometimes up to ten feet, with their beaks and claws and then hollow out a chamber at the end where the eggs are laid. The young birds are often brought up on a bed of old fish scales and bones.

Bottom left This is one of the most beautiful of all bird's nests, and is undoubtedly the work of a master-builder —the Long-tailed Tit. The nest is a lovely, oval structure with thick walls made of moss and lichen, strengthened by spiders' webs and hairs, and has a small, slit-like entrance. The lining is of silky, fluffy feathers, which may number anything up to 2,000. Warm and strong, it really is the ideal home of the bird world, and houses sometimes up to twelve young.

Right A Swallow's mud nest stuck onto a corner of the roof in a barn. The birds can sometimes be seen collecting mud from ponds and fields, and the nest is lined with grasses. Swallows usually choose a barn or farm building, and occasionally a bridge to build their nest, but House Martins, which closely resemble Swallows, often nest on the side of houses and under the eaves so that their nest and young can be seen quite clearly.

Above These Chinstrap Penguins—so called because of the black stripe running from behind the eye down under the chin to the other eye—are unusual in that they build more elaborate nests than most Penguins, consisting of a large pile of rocks to hold the eggs. A great deal of squabbling goes on in the colonies over the selection of stones, and there is much stealing from other nests.

Left A beautiful photograph of the incredible nest of the Indian Tailorbird. The pocket made of two leaves joined together with strong hairs can be clearly seen one on each side of the sausage-like nest which is woven out of feathers and down.

Right The beautiful Black Tern of North America and Eurasia builds a solid nest of sticks and any floating vegetation it can find, and this one is firmly wedged in between rushes and roots. The chicks have very attractive brown and white colouring and are white and grey in colour for the whole of their first year, in striking contrast to the sooty plumage of the adult birds.

Left White Storks would not win a prize for tidy nest building, but perhaps chimneys and roof tops are not the easiest of places to nest. . . . They are encouraged to build wherever they like, because of the superstitious belief that they bring good luck to a household, and they are a common sight in villages in eastern Europe, although they are not as numerous as they once were.

Below Bee-eaters are some of the most brilliantly coloured of all birds, and this is a Rainbow Bee-eater flying to its nest tunnel in the ground with a beakful of food. The birds dig tunnels of anything up to six feet in the sand and lay their eggs in a chamber at the end, which is lined with the remains of the bees and wasps that they eat.

Right The male New World Humming-birds are the true jewels of the bird world, and as might be suspected from their shining splendour and special courting plumage, they are not model husbands. It is the dully-plumaged female who builds the tiny, intricate nest of spiders' webs, lichens and soft plant down, often placed on top of a branch or in the fork between two branches. This is a female Ruby-throated Hummingbird, the common, and only, Hummer of eastern North America, feeding its young on nectar.

Below A Pheasant's nest in the under-growth of a hedge full of the beautiful oval eggs.

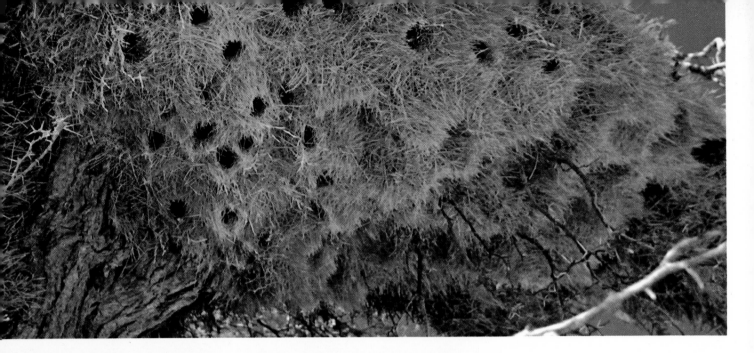

Above Not a monstrous growth of fungus . . . but the astonishing and complex nests of the Sociable Weaver of South Africa. The entrances of the nests are at the bottom (the photograph is taken looking up at the structure) and each pair of birds uses only its own nest, although they all help with repairs to the roof when necessary, Moreover, the couples would seem to be very faithful to each other although they live so close to hundreds of other birds.

Left The male Crimson Chat, a species of the eastern parts of Australia and West Australia is a brightly coloured bird which could not fail to attract the attention of any nature-lover. The nest is made of grass and twigs lined with hair and normally concealed in a low bush.

Right Love and attention for a female Goldfinch in the form of a nice fat bug from her mate. Such courtship feeding is quite common, as it both cements the pair bond and means that the eggs are not left to get cold. Goldfinches are the most glamorous of all the finches and have brilliant yellow bars on their wings which flash gold as the birds flit through the trees.

Left This Mallee Fowl is one of the Megapodes of southern Australia which all incubate their eggs in a heap of sand and rotting vegetation.

Below Bird on a floating island—this well-made nest exactly fits the shape of the handsome Great Northern Diver, or Common Loon, as it is known in North America, which is its main nesting area. Loons don't always build 'islands', but sometimes just line a hollow on land with moss.

Right A Blue-necked Tanager is one of a large family which lives in the tropical parts of the Americas. They all build fairly similar cup shaped nests which are loosely woven together with anything they can find.

Wildfowl and Wetland Birds

For centuries wildfowl have been one of the most popular groups of birds. Firstly they are highly valued as food, and duck shooting is a favourite pastime of sportsmen all over the world. Then many of them are very attractive, having unusual and beautiful colouring, others are often of imposing size, and are a magnificent sight in flight, while some have distinctive cries which carry across the flat swamps for many miles. Their habitat, which is principally marshes and wetlands, is a beautiful and wild type of country, which has appealed to many artists, and the reed beds and fields are not complete without a flock of swans or geese or duck flying in the well-known 'v' formation across the sky.

The domesticated members of the three main groups of wildfowl—swans, geese and ducks—are so well-known that many people do not realize that there are 145 different species, and that the farmyard ducks and geese are descended from the world's commonest wild duck, the Mallard, and the wild Greylag Goose which breeds right across Europe and Asia. There are many different types of duck—among them the Shelducks, which are almost like small geese; the Dipping Ducks, which are by far the largest group of waterfowl and include the common Black Duck, a sportsman's favourite in North America which domesticates very easily; the Perching Ducks that spend more time in trees than any of the others and include three of the most brilliantly coloured of the waterfowl, the Mandarin Duck of eastern Asia and Japan, the closely related Wood Duck of North America, and the popular Muscovy Duck; and others like the Eider Ducks, the Mergansers and the Stiff-tailed Ducks. One or two do not fit into any particular group such as the Torrent Duck, which lives in the swift-flowing mountain streams in the Andes and is an excellent swimmer. It is expert at either going upstream against very strong currents or at travelling down stream at tremendous speed and steering skilfully with its stiff, horny tail feathers to avoid rocks. In Australia the beautiful Pink-eared Duck lives on stretches of shallow water on the plains, and has an enormous spoon-shaped bill with membraneous flaps hanging down outside at the tip of it.

There are many other birds which live with the wildfowl in wetlands, and the great flocks of mixed birds flying or feeding over marshes and swamps are a splendid sight. They are nearly all very gregarious and live in large colonies. During the migrating season yet more birds often stop off at large wetland areas on their way to their winter quarters, so that sometimes hundreds of thousands of many different types can be seen together. Herons are silent and stately inhabitants of estuaries, lakes and swamps, and nest in surrounding trees or reeds, as do the Spoonbills that are found in south eastern America and Eurasia. Relatives of theirs are the Ibises, and the Scarlet Ibis which lives in South America rivals the magnificent Flamingoes in beauty and colouring. Storks are a very ancient species which are found all over the world and have for centuries been regarded as an omen of good luck, particularly by the Teutonic peoples. This superstition has protected them on their breeding grounds and enabled so large and striking a bird as the White Stork to be still so common today. One of the most interesting is the Shoebill Stork, found in the papyrus marshes of the Upper Nile and its tributaries. It has a grotesque beak almost as wide as it is long apparently adapted for catching lungfish and gars, its favourite food, and also frogs, young turtles and crocodiles and small mammals.

Cranes are another group of large and handsome birds which inhabit the wetlands and are sadly in need of protection, though a smaller relative of theirs, the Limpkin, which was at one time in danger of dying out, has since been afforded protection and is now quite common again. Limpkins are found throughout the Americas, and are so called because of their limping gait; a common nickname for them is 'Crying birds' after their loud, wailing cry most often heard at evening and at night. They feed on freshwater snails which they wedge between tree roots or stones to crack the shell and extract the snail. They have exceptionally long toes for running over water lilies and other swamp vegetation. The Jacanas, or 'Lilytrotters' are also expert at walking on the water, as their name suggests, and are found in Africa and America.

Waders are very attractive birds,

principally of the Northern Hemisphere, and are mainly small with long legs and beaks specially adapted to help them obtain their food in the shallow mud of marshes and shores. The beaks are sometimes almost as long as the birds and can turn up, down and even sideways, like that of the New Zealand Wrybill. Curlews have very long, down-curving beaks with which they probe for worms in the mud; the best known are the Hudsonian Curlew of America and the Eurasian Curlew and both migrate considerable distances. Oystercatchers are attractive birds easily identified by their bright red bills and legs, as are the North American Dowitchers which have brilliant red breasts in spring and fly in large flocks along coastal mud-

flats and beaches in winter. Stilts have extremely long legs and long, straight bills, and the Banded Stilt of Australia is a particularly striking species with distinctive black, white and chesnut colouring and beautiful pink legs. Together with the Avocets they are true wetland birds, wading through muddy waters probing for food and able to swim and fly strongly. The Sandpipers, Sanderlings, Plovers and Turnstones feed in small colonies or groups, calling to each other as they work their way steadily along the beaches and marshes in search of food. They all travel in large, loose flocks, and the Sandpipers can turn and wheel in unison when playing over their feeding grounds although there is no apparent 'leader' or formation

among the hundreds of birds.

There is always a fear that all these birds will become increasingly rare because their habitat is one of those that is threatened perhaps more than any other by the march of civilization. The regular reclaiming of land for building and farming purposes has meant that swamps, marshes and lakes are already so reduced in number that very often they are seriously overcrowded by the waterfowl, waders and the migrant passers-by. Some of the large swamps in Holland and Germany can be the most marvellous places to watch the birds, because they house so many thousands, but it is very important that they should be protected as they are of vital importance to the lives of a great many species.

Previous page: left An American Avocet feeds in shallow water in North Dakota. They are fond of shallow, muddy pools where they wade slowly and sedately, lifting their legs deliberately one after the other. They sweep their long, upturned bills from side to side in a wide arc either at the surface or near the bottom of the water with mandibles slightly open to trap small animals.

Right The attractive and friendly Greylag Goose is the wild relation of the farmyard goose.

Top left Among Africa's many and varied birds one of the oddest-looking is the Hammerkop or Hammerhead. It is a heron-like bird, and gets its name from the horizontal long crest on the back of its head which resembles the nail-pulling end of a hammer. Rather stolid birds, they can suddenly start to gambol, jumping round and bowing to each other in an awkward fashion before retiring to their accustomed solemnity.

Centre left The conspicuous white bill and forehead of the Coot have given the bird the alternative name of 'Baldpate'. They are aggressive birds and frequently fight in spring, chasing each other over the water with their feet pattering furiously on the surface and spray flying up around them. All good swimmers, they spend most of their time on open water, nodding their heads as they travel rapidly from reed bed to reed bed. In winter they gather into large flocks and inhabit both fresh and brackish coastal waters.

Bottom left An African Jacana about to settle down and brood its eggs. The nest is a mass of floating loose vegetation, and the eggs are particularly beautiful, being a dark, glossy brown, spotted and blotched with black. After the breeding season the birds fly in small flocks over lakes and marshes in the way that so many waders do.

Right The Mandarin Duck is one of the most popular of all wildfowl, no doubt because of its magnificent plumage. The female is rather dull in her grey and brown colours but the male is surely one of the world's most attractive birds, especially with his striking orange 'sails'.

Left Part of a huge flock of Shoveler, with a few Pintail, resting on an Indian lake. This beautiful duck breeds right across Europe and Asia and part of North America. The large spatulate bill of the Shoveler contains fine filters which act as a sieve when the bird feeds, which it does by swimming with its bill half under water and sucking as it goes along.

Below One of the commonest ducks in the Northern Hemisphere is the Northern Pintail. The males are extremely handsome and are also easy to keep in a wildfowl collection. The females are duller, being a mottled brown, but have the same slender shape as the drakes and slightly pointed tail.

Right A collection of waders... Oyster-catchers, Herring Gulls, Curlews, Cormorants and Bar-tailed Godwits feeding in the rock pools at the edge of the sea.

Below Lesser Flamingoes.... Their remarkably long legs and necks are perhaps best seen when they fly, which they do in long skeins, necks and legs stretched out straight. They are vocal in flight, honking much like geese.

Above An American Limpkin demonstrates how well camouflaged it can be in its habitat of marshes and swampland —it prefers to keep hidden, whether it is perched in trees, wading through dense vegetation or swimming along streams.

Left In the Florida Everglades, an excellent place for watching birds, America's largest Heron may be seen on the mangrove islands. The American Great White Heron is very shy, though it is possible to catch the bird unawares as it stands motionless in the water waiting for frogs or fish to pass within striking distance or perhaps, as in this picture, standing with its wings held out in a characteristic wing-sunning posture.

Right The Canada Goose is a fine example of a bird that has been successfully introduced into new areas. In the seventeenth century it was brought into England and has since spread all over Great Britain and is also breeding in Northern Ireland and in Sweden.

Migration

The migration of birds is a very complex and interesting subject, and one which we still do not entirely understand. Many birds travel hundreds of miles twice a year in order to have a consistent supply of food and avoid cold weather. Thus migration is a seasonal mass movement which has largely become instinctive in most birds, and part of their annual cycle of courtship, nesting, rearing the young and moulting; though the behaviour undoubtedly originated as a means of securing the best available food supply at a given time. Vast numbers of birds breed in the northern regions and in the Arctic where the summer brings a glut of insects and fish to feed the ravenous youngsters. They then move south before the onset of the northern winter when the fish would be frozen under the water, the insects die off and the weather would be too cold for the birds to survive. In the Southern Hemisphere the reverse is true, and birds like the Long-tailed Cuckoo nest in New Zealand and then move north for their off season. Other birds make tremendous journeys from east to west, such as the Arctic and Siberian Warblers, and even Penguins migrate by tobogganing and walking over the pack ice.

One of the most astonishing things in the bird world is the length and speed of many of these transequatorial journeys, often undertaken by quite small birds. The Artic Tern and the Sharp-tailed Shearwater, or Muttonbird, both cover about 11,000 miles twice a year, and are perhaps the most celebrated long distance travellers of all. The Ruby-throated Hummingbird buzzes non-stop for 500 to 1,000 miles across the Gulf of Mexico, and many small Warblers also have the capacity to fly for days without resting or feeding and cross the Sahara Desert in one go. The American Golden Plover flies direct from its Canadian breeding grounds to winter in Hawaii, an incredible journey of 2,000 miles. These 'long haul' travellers are capable of completing their journeys, or part of their journeys, in a staggeringly short time, a Blue-winged Teal, has been known to average 125 miles a day, and a Knot (a British wading bird) covered 3,500 miles in 8 days.

The amazing migration route of the graceful Arctic Tern was revealed fifty years ago by the recoveries of young Terns that had been ringed on their breeding grounds and later recovered off the Cape coast. The birds breed completely around the Northern Hemisphere from as far south as Cape Cod, where a few Arctic Terns nest with the vast colonies of Common Terns, to as far north as northern Greenland on the Atlantic coast, and in Europe from northern Britain to the Siberian coast. The Terns fly southward to winter in the waters off South Africa and the Antarctic—those nesting in north eastern Siberia and Alaska fly down to the eastern Pacific, and those nesting in North America head firstly north east to join others from the northern breeding colonies along the Labrador coast, and then swing round in a great circle across the Atlantic to fly south down the west coast of Europe and Africa. They live to a great age in spite of all this travelling, and it is an Arctic Tern that holds the longevity record among Terns—one ringed in Norway as a chick died on the same ternery twenty seven years later.

There is an unusual type of migration which is performed by Waxwings. They usually travel south in winter, but they have no fixed territories or regular places where they can be counted upon to reappear every year. At four to seven year intervals huge flocks of Waxwings 'erupt' southward far beyond their normal wintering range into regions where they are virtually unknown, and many of the birds are too exhausted to return to breed in the spring after such a long journey. It used to be thought that this extraordinary form of migration was caused by the insufficient number of berries, which they eat in vast quantities, in their usual habitats, but it now seems that the migration is a way of controlling the population of the species, as many of the birds never return to the north.

How do these birds accomplish these great distances without feeding on the way and how do they manage to navigate so accurately? The start of it all is the gradual shortening of the days in early autumn, when migrating species, which are extremely sensitive to the changing hours of daylight, begin to lay up reserves of fat and become restless and often very sociable. The end of the summer is heralded by the sight of masses of Swallows and House Martins collecting on the telephone wires, and in North America the Bobolinks do likewise. Instinctively they know when the weather conditions are favourable for a long journey south, and vast flocks will suddenly leave over night on the start of their travels. Much more puzzling is how the birds find their way, sometimes to exactly the same spot each year without hesitation and in some cases, such as that of young Cuckoos, without any company or tuition. It is apparent from various experiments that birds must have a very accurate means of telling where they are on the earth in relation to their nest or their destination—for instance a Manx Shearwater removed from its burrow in Wales and released at Boston Airport made the return journey of 3,050 miles to the burrow in twelve and a half days, and this was from a strange part of the world where it would never normally go. It seems most likely that birds navigate by using the sun and the stars, (which means that they also have an accurate sense of timing), and this explains why migrants become disorientated in fog and bad weather.

The most successful method of discovering where birds migrate and how fast they fly has been ringing, which has been in use for nearly a hundred years. Millions of different birds have been ringed and a large proportion of them recovered months and sometimes years later on the other side of the world. Recently ornithologists have been using high powered radar equipment, which has for the first time revealed how many birds travel by night, and also the great height at which most birds fly. It would seem that many of the birds seen at sea level or from the ground are stragglers or 'lost' ones that do not accurately represent what the rest of the species is doing. However, even if one cannot draw scientific conclusions from the passing flocks of migrating birds, they still give those watching them great

pleasure, and it is an inspiring sight when thousands of Starlings or Chaffinches or Bramblings wing their way up into the air in great, black flocks to make their way south before winter comes.

There is much to be learned about migration, since it is not known how the birds manage to compensate for drift, or how the young birds migrating for the first time manage to keep up with the adults. Experiments have shown that the adult birds who have done the journey before are better at finding their way than the young ones, if blown off course or forcibly removed from their usual route; on the other hand the juveniles

can take up the correct course without any apparent trouble. Even more remarkable are the young birds whose parents leave several weeks before them and which have to find their own way to places quite unknown to them, forced on by instinct and inherited expertise. Young Cuckoos and Sharp-tailed Shearwaters from Australia are left by their parents to find their own way to their winter quarters, although they are only a few months old, have very small brains, and have no knowledge of where they are going. The migration of birds is certainly one of the most fascinating of all the unexplained natural phenomenons.

Previous page: left A beautiful Arctic Tern soaring off on one of its 11,000 mile journeys. Their navigation is extremely accurate as they return every year to exactly the same breeding grounds.

Right These Snow Geese are migrating southwards seeking warmer weather for the winter. They breed circumpolarly in the very high north, flying down to the United States, Europe and Japan to wintering grounds which are now very often protected areas. Although ungainly on land, they are impressive in the air.

———

Below Swallows and Martins gather together before migrating . . . contrary to the custom of the majority of migrating birds they travel by day, and ringing has shown that birds from central Europe winter in tropical Africa, while those that breed in Britain tend to go further south to the Cape Province and Natal.

Right A Waxwing looking as if it is ready to leave its breeding grounds and find warmer weather elsewhere. These attractive little birds are found across northern Eurasia and North America, and are highly gregarious, migrating and breeding in close-knit flocks.

Left A beautiful Bluethroat shows off its brilliant colours as it alights at the nest . . . one of the Thrush family, it migrates from northern Eurasia to winter in the tropics. It has been known to cross the Bering Sea to nest in north western America, but it still returns in the autmun to Eurasia to follow the traditional flyways to its winter quarters.

Below Hummingbirds have perhaps the most remarkable powers of flight of any bird, and are second to none in agility. They have supreme mastery of movement in the air, being able to hover motionless, fly backwards, sideways, or straight up and down, their wings moving so fast that they are invisible to humans and make the humming noise that give them their name. Twice a year this Ruby-throated Hummer from California crosses the Gulf of Mexico to spend the winter in a warmer climate.

Right This Long-tailed Cuckoo from New Zealand has an amazing migration route. Rather than travel up the east coast of Australia and New Guinea, it crosses between two and three thousand miles of ocean to reach its wintering grounds in the Ellice, Society, Solomon and Fiji islands.

Birds of Prey

The birds of prey are one of the most impressive groups of birds in the world, and they have captured the imagination of many people throughout history from Caesar downwards. This is probably because of their great power, evident in the hooked beaks, the fierce eyes, and the strong talons which enable them to capture their prey in dramatic and devastating style. It is also partly due to the fact that an aura has grown up around them because they are seen so rarely, and are instantly recognizable when they do appear by their distinctive flight and ominous hovering over the land in search of some unsuspecting animal. Moreover, man has been more successful in training Falcons than any other bird, and hawking has been a popular sport since the Middle Ages.

There are really two distinct types, or orders, of birds of prey: the diurnal birds of prey or Falconiformes, and the Owls, or Strigiformes. Although many of both orders are very large, powerful birds, a number are extremely small. The Red-thighed Falconet from South East Asia is about the same size as a Sparrow, and the Elf Owl from Mexico and south west United States is even smaller. However, the Falconet and the other Pygmy Falcons are true birds of prey and are capable of killing birds as large

as themselves, and even in some cases birds twice their size.

The Falconiformes vary according to their habitats and ways of life. Vultures, which fly many miles during the day in search of dead animals, have long broad wings which enable them to soar easily and glide for hours on the currents in the hot air. These are a handicap when it comes to taking off from the ground, but they lack the dash and strength of the typical raptors in any case, and seldom attack prey that might offer any resistance, eating partly rotten flesh in comfort on the ground before taking to the air again at their leisure. Eagles and Buzzards have wings that are shorter and narrower than those of the Vultures, and tails which are longer and much stronger and which act as rudders. The birds can still soar without difficulty, but are also able to chase and swoop after their prey and catch it on the ground before it escapes, which requires great agility and accuracy of movement.

Harriers have yet longer and narrower wings and even longer tails, and hunt by gliding low over reed-beds or open country and suddenly dropping onto their prey, taking it by surprise, rather than giving chase. The swiftest birds of all are the Falcons. Their wings are broad-based, but taper to a long

thin point, and this enables them to fly at great speed after their prey, which is not on the ground but in the air and the most difficult to catch. They can also soar, but not as well as eagles and vultures, and some use this ability to gain height above other birds and then dive at incredible speed to knock them out of the air. The accuracy and speed of this manoeuvre, which is called stooping and is a speciality of the Peregrine Falcon, makes it a breathtaking spectacle to watch. The dives are made at incredible speed, and have been measured as exceeding 200 miles per hour in some cases. If they are accurate, as they usually are, the prey is killed instantly and is knocked out of the air, while the Peregrine circles up and round and comes back to feast at its leisure. Unfortunately, the use of pesticides on agricultural land has reduced the numbers of these birds considerably and they are now rare in the United States where they once used to be common birds.

There are also a couple of rather famous birds of prey that do not fit into the other categories because of their differing anatomies and lifestyles—the Osprey and the African Secretarybird. The Osprey looks like the rest of the Hawks, but has its own adaptations to enable it to catch live fish in a very expert manner. Soaring in circles over the water until it sights a fish, it hovers for a moment and then plunges down feet first and often goes under the water completely while it grasps the fish tightly with both talons. Struggling clear of the surface it goes off to a tree or a rock to eat its prey. The talons have spikey scales on the under surface and the four toes are of equal length and reversible as they are in owls. Ospreys are now re-established in Scotland, after rather too much publicity when they first returned in 1958, and it is hoped that their numbers will increase there.

The Secretarybird is even more peculiar and has exceptionally long legs for running through the grass lands. It feeds on snakes which it catches by rushing at them while protecting itself with its wings, and then stamping on them behind the head until they are dead. Snakes that are too big to kill in this fashion it carries into the air and then drops on the hard ground.

The Owls do not immediately strike one as having any close resemblance to the raptors but they in fact hunt the same prey, and consequently have the same hooked beaks, keen eyesight and strong talons as the raptors. Many owls can be very fierce indeed, even though their soft plumage and round baby faces belie any such idea. All the Owls' peculiarities probably stem from the fact that they are nocturnal —their silent flight, forward-looking eyes, and particularly large ears are all aids to flying and hunting at night in the dark. They are a much more uniform group than the raptors with short, broad wings and short tails as they do not soar. They hunt by waiting absolutely still in a well hidden spot until an unsuspecting animal or bird comes out into the open unaware that there is anything near. Then they dart out and seize their quarry, returning to their perch to eat it.

Most of the birds of prey and almost all the owls prefer to live in pairs and have their own territory where they find all their food and which they defend against any competitors. Owls tend to be very possessive and mercilessly attack intruders throughout most of the year. Others of the birds of prey are less concerned about their territories outside the breeding season and do not bother to take up a territory in their winter quarters. One of the reasons why the birds of prey are, as a group, growing increasingly rare is that the young birds, after they become independent of their parents, are often unable to find a territory and are not sufficiently experienced to catch enough food. On the other hand those that survive will live to a ripe old age, the larger species surviving for forty years or more.

Previous page: left In the Old World the Black Kite has a very extensive distribution and is well-known in many parts for its scavenging habits especially in Africa where this picture was taken. Kites are masterful fliers and are very graceful as they glide in a leisurely fashion with occasional slow wing beats and continuous turns of the tail. Although the Black Kite is fond of carrion and also kills its own food—rabbits, mice, voles, reptiles, and young birds—one of its favourite meals is fish. Wherever there are lakes or rivers any Black Kite in the vicinity will often be found at the edge of the water picking up dead and dying fish.

Right The Brown Falcon is a well-known bird of prey in Australia and New Guinea, and is quite a large bird though it often hunts from a perch instead of using its power and speed in the air. It is very varied in colouring which is a common characteristic of many birds of prey.

Top left The Hen Harrier is a typical Harrier which lives in North America and Eurasia, and is known in the New World as the Marsh Hawk. Instead of having the incredibly sharp eyesight common to most of the birds of prey, Harriers have very good hearing, and find their prey by listening for the slightest sound of its presence in the field below them. This is why they have faces like those of the owls, because their large ear-openings are protected by feather ruffs.

Left An adult male Great Horned Owl calls from a dead tree stump. This species occurs from northern Canada right through to the south of South America and is one of the largest and most agressive of its family. It is very useful in controlling the number of pests and regularly takes rabbits, mice and squirrels.

Right As it returns to its nest a Boobook Owl shows its boldly barred underwing. Also known as the Morepork Owl, which is, as is Boobook, an imitation of its call, it is resident in Australia, New Zealand and on some of the nearby islands. It feeds by night on insects, small mammals and small birds.

Left Secretarybirds are alleged to have got their name from the quill-like feathers at the back of their necks which resemble feather pens stuck behind the ear of a typical old time clerk. These are long legged hawks found in the African grasslands and are placed in a family of their own because they are so unlike the rest of their order.

Below The Short-eared Owl is an inhabitant of open country, building its nest on the ground in marshy areas. It is found across Eurasia and much of the New World and is often seen during the day and at dusk quartering the ground in the manner of a Harrier in search of small mammals.

Right Although not a true bird of prey scientifically, the Shrike is similar in appearance and habits. This is a male Red-backed Shrike, which breeds in Europe and Asia and winters in Africa and Arabia. Its diet includes insects, small mammals and small birds which it stores by impaling on thorns in a favourite spot called a 'larder'.

Below A pair of young Tawny Owls, just out of the nest, wait on a branch to be fed. Brown or Wood Owls, as they are also called, are probably the best known owls in Europe, and they are the birds that utter the pleasant hooting call which is familiar to most Europeans and can be heard all the year round, and especially in autumn and winter when the birds are claiming their territories.

Above Young Barn Owls which still have their creamy white down. Barn Owls are found on every continent, and are possibly the most widespread of all the owls; they can often be seen at dusk as a white shape flying low over the ground. They also have a repertoire of rather strange noises which includes hisses, snores, bill-snapping, short cries and a long-drawn out shriek which has a decidedly eerie quality about it.

Left An Osprey returns to its nest. Like the Peregrine Falcon this bird is found throughout the world, although it does not breed in South America but is a winter visitor there. A large, powerful, soaring and flapping hawk, it feeds almost entirely on fish, and because of its adaptions to enable it to catch its prey, it is placed by ornithologists in a family of its own.

Right A magnificent Peregrine Falcon at its nest. These are among the most accomplished flyers of all and probably because of this they are the most numerous of the birds of prey and are found on all continents of the world.

Left The Bald Eagle was made the national bird of the United States in 1782, and is a striking bird with a white head and tail. During the present century it has become very rare and has completely disappeared from most of its previous haunts. Destruction of its habitat and poisoning from pesticides, besides the indiscriminate and irresponsible shooting which is still practised illegally, are the principal causes for its decline, but with luck and the protection of the law its status should now gradually improve.

Below The Crowned Hawk Eagle of Africa is one of the most powerful birds in the world, and is found only in the forests south of the Sahara, where it feeds on mammals up to the size of

bushbucks and antelopes. It has an impressive double crest which it raises when angry or excited and at such times its staring yellow eyes give it an extremely frightening aspect as this photograph shows.

Right The Bateleur is one of the strangest of eagles in shape and in its life style. The wings are long and broad and enable the Bateleur to spend hours gliding in the air without flapping its wings—it uses the warm up-currents of air in the open country of its home in tropical Africa and may cover anything up to 200 miles on the lookout for reptiles and small prey.

Left The Common Kestrel is the most numerous falcon in Europe, Asia and Africa, and the Nankeen Kestrel, right, is very similar to it, replacing it in Australia and New Guinea. Both pictures are of female birds at their respective nests, which may be built on a ledge or in a hole in a tree or wall, or even in an old nest of some other bird. They rarely bother to build a nest proper, and the young birds are brought up on a mat of regurgitated pellets.

Below This cross and scruffy looking Eaglet does not look as if it belongs to one of the most noble species of them all—the Golden Eagle, symbol, since the Roman Empire, of strength and reliability. However, young Golden Eagles take about four years to attain full adult plumage, which is any shade of brown with a golden or straw coloured patch on the back of the neck. They are mountain dwellers throughout most of the Northern Hemisphere.

Acknowledgements

The publishers would like to thank the following individuals and organizations for their kind permission to reproduce the pictures in this book:

A M Anderson *Natural History Photographic Agency* 12 top, 33; Ronald Austing *Frank Lane* 34, 41 top, 58 bottom, 62 bottom, 68; Douglas Baglin *NHPA* 30 bottom; Hans and Judy Beste *Ardea* 5; R M Bloomfield *Ardea* 48 bottom; Joe B Blossom *NHPA* 13; J B and S Bottomley *Ardea* 48 centre; G J Broekhuysen *Ardea* 42 top; Arthur Christiansen *Frank Lane* Title page, contents page, 20/21, 27, 32 top, 66 bottom; *Bruce Coleman* 8 top, 10 top and centre, 14 top, 18, 22 top, 23, 30 top, 31, 38 bottom, 40 top, 43, 46, 51 bottom, 52 bottom, 56, 65 top; *Colour Library International* 17, 24 centre, 50 bottom, 59, 65 bottom; Werner Curth *Ardea* 9; Norman Duerden *Frank Lane* 67; Whitney Eastman 6 bottom, 52 top; Harry Engels *Frank Lane* 16 bottom; M D England *Ardea* 44 top, 50 top; Kenneth Fink *Ardea* 61, 66 top; Alan Foley *Associated Freelance Artists* 71; Mike Harris 24 top, 32 bottom; Brian Hawkes *NHPA* 48 top; E H Herbert *AFA* 7, 8 bottom, 37, 38 top, 39; H Hoflinger *Frank Lane* 28 bottom; Eric Hosking 4, 14 bottom, 15, 29, 36 top, 41 bottom, 51 top, 54, 55, 64 top, 68/69; W J Howes *AFA* 12 bottom; Geoffrey Kinns *AFA* 70 bottom; P Knowles *AFA* 42 bottom; Frank Lane 16 top; Don MacCaskill *AFA* 57, 62 top, 70 top; John Marchington *Ardea* 53; G H Moon *Frank Lane* 24 bottom, 63; Pat Morris *Ardea* 69; Georg Nystrand *Frank Lane* 28 top; YSIBOY Photopress *Frank Lane* 6 top; Graham Pizzey *NHPA* 10 bottom, 11; S Roberts *Ardea* 47; C P Rose *Frank Lane* 44 bottom; Heinz Schrempp *Frank Lane* 45, 49, 64 bottom; Wilf Taylor *Ardea* 40 bottom; Ronald Thompson *Frank Lane* 25, 36 bottom; Teuvo Suominen *AFA* 58 top; John Wightman *Ardea* 60; Tom Willock *Ardea* 26; Renato Zanatta *AFA* 19, 23 bottom; D Zingel *Frank Lane* 35.